SAFE PAWS

A Dog Owners Guide to Snake Avoidance Without the Use of Shock or Punishment

Penny DiLoreto

"A dog has no use for fancy cars, big homes, or designer clothes. A waterlogged stick will do just fine. A dog doesn't care if you're rich or poor, educated or illiterate, clever or dull. Give him your heart and he will give you his."

JOHN GROGAN

CONTENTS

FOREWORD

"Pioneering dog expert Penny DiLoreto is a true leader in snake avoidance alternatives for dog-loving people looking for a method that works but does not justify harm to their beloved dogs. The public outcry and need for force-free, snake-avoidance training without the use of shock are at long last answered here. Bravo!"
- Linda Michaels, M.A., Psychology Creator of the Hierarchy of Dog Needs.

"Penny DiLoreto's Force Free Snake Avoidance Training has been a lifesaver for my clients. Living in the high desert of Nevada exposes my clients and their dogs to rattlesnakes not just on hikes and walks but in their backyards. It is a blessing and a relief to be able to offer them a humane and safe alternative to shock collars. Thank you for your work!
- Sarah Anderson, MA Ed., CPDT-KA

PREFACE

When I set out to write Safe Paws, my main goal was to help dog owners like you protect their furry friends from the dangers of sake encounters. Living in an area with venomous snakes, I know firsthand the anxiety and fear that come with the threat of snakebites.

This book brings together years of research, training, and collaboration with veterinary experts and snake specialists to provide you with the best information and practical advice.

Safe Paws is much more than just a training guide. It includes detailed information about different snake species, their habitats, and behaviors. I've also included interviews with veterinarians who share their insights on treating snakebites, along with tips on preventative measures. My hope is to give you the knowledge and tools you need to keep your dog safe and healthy.

I owe a huge thanks to Dr. Karen Seibold, DVM, and Dr. Janet Moston, DVM, whose veterinary expertise has been invaluable. A special shout-out to Tom Derr for his fascinating insights into snake behavior and safety and to my family and friends for their unwavering support and encouragement throughout this project.

Writing this book has been a labor of love. It serves as a valuable resource for all dog owners, helping you to ensure the safety and well-being of your four-legged companions. Thank you for joining me on this journey to protect our beloved pets.

Warm regards,
Penny DiLoreto, CPDT-KA

PROLOGUE

As the sun was setting, casting long shadows across the landscape, the faint rattle of a snake could be heard. A stark reminder of the hidden dangers lurking in the underbrush.

Anna's dog Lucy bonded down the hiking trail ahead of her, nose to the ground, oblivious to the dangers that lay just a few feet away. Suddenly, a sharp yelp pierced the air.

Anna's heart raced as she saw Lucy leap back, her paw raised and trembling. She had found the source of the rattle-a venomous rattlesnake coiled and ready to strike.

Panic set in as Anna rushed to her dog's side, knowing that every second counted. She scooped Lucy up and ran back to her car. Her mind was a whirlwind of fear and urgency. The next few hours were a blur of frantic activity, a desperate race to get Lucy the help she needed.

The vet's office was miles away, and Anna drove as fast as she could, praying for her dog's safety as Lucy whimpered softly, her eyes filled with confusion and pain.

The vets worked quickly, administering antivenom and stabilizing Lucy's condition. It was a close call, but Lucy pulled through.

This terrifying experience was a wake-up call for my friend Anna. It highlighted the importance of training and preparedness, not just for Lucy but for all dogs living in snake-prone areas.

Safe Paws was born from testimonies like Anna's. My desire to create a comprehensive guide to equip dog owners with the training, knowledge, and tools needed to protect their beloved pets from the dangers of snakes while enjoying the outdoors.

In the pages that follow, you will find everything you need to know to keep your dog safe, from identiyfing different snake species to training techniques and emergency medical treatment advice.

Let this book be your guide in ensuring the safety and well-being of your furry friend.

INTRODUCTION

The threat of snakebites is a serious concern for dog owners, especially in areas where venomous snakes are common. *Safe Paws* is designed to equip you with the knowledge and tools needed to protect your beloved pet from these dangers.

This book covers a wide range of topics, from effective training techniques to essential medical treatments and understanding snake behavior. In the following chapters, you'll learn about various snake species, their habitats, and how to identify them.

We will delve into practical training methods to teach your dog to avoid snakes, supported by interviews with experienced veterinarians and snake experts. You'll also find comprehensive information on the medical protocols for treating snakebites, along with preventative measures to minimize risks.

Whether you're a seasoned dog owner or new to pet care, Safe Paws provides valuable insights and actionable steps to ensure your dog's safety. By the end of this book, you'll feel confident in our ability to protect your pet fom snake encounters and handle any emergencies that may arise.

Join me on this journey to safeguard our furry friends and give them the safe, happy lives they deserve. Together, we can make sure our dogs stay safe, healthy, and free from the dangers of snakebites.

Warm regards.
Penny DiLoreto, CPDT-KA

THANK YOU

Thank you for choosing, "Safe Paws." You may also like other books I have written on the topic of dog training. **Scan the QR code below** to sign up for my FREE Preferred Readers Club. Members receive:

* Free Book Give-A-Ways.
* Advanced notices of new releases
* The chance to win exciting prizes.

Or visit my blog at:

Dog Eared Diaries.com

SECTION 1   BUILDING
THE FOUNDATION

CHAPTER 1: A KINDER PATH

Developing the Force-Free Snake Avoidance Program

"THE GREATNESS OF A NATION AND ITS MORAL PROGRESS CAN
BE JUDGED BY THE WAY ITS ANIMALS ARE TREATED." — MAHATMA
GANDHI

In 2011, I developed the Force-Free Snake Avoidance Program, a major step in my journey as a dog trainer. This idea came to life after my dog had a scary run-in with a snake in our backyard.

That incident made me determined to find a snake-avoidance dog training program my dog could attend in my area.

However, I was disappointed to discover that all the programs I looked into relied heavily on shock collars and harsh methods —approaches that really went against my belief in kindness and positive reinforcement.

Determined to find a better solution, I threw myself into research. I talked with professional snake handlers, veterinarians, and other trainers to learn all I could about snake behavior and dog training methods that would be safe for both snakes and dogs.

Through trial and error and a lot of collaborative effort, my "Force-Free Snake Avoidance Program" was born. It offers a safe, stress-free way for dogs to learn to avoid snakes without fear or pain.

In the following pages, you'll find simple training steps that are not only effective but also strengthen the loving bond you share with your dog. It's all about making sure your adventurous companion can enjoy every outing safely, giving you peace of mind.

Little Known Facts: Did you know that snakes shed their skin multiple times a year, a process known as ecdysis, to allow for growth and to remove parasites?

In my Force Free Snake Avoidance Class, I use shed snake skin that I've found on walks, received from friends who have pet snakes, and gotten from my local reptile store.

CHAPTER 2: PREPARE FOR TRAINING

Equipment and Supplies

Before you begin teaching your dog to avoid snakes, it's best to prepare both yourself and your furry friend for the training ahead. In this chapter, I'll cover everything you need to get started, including the equipment, ensuring a safe training environment, and the steps to get your dog ready.

By taking the time to prepare thoroughly, you'll create a positive training experience that both you and your dog will enjoy.

Like with any training, it's important to have the right equipment. Having the right tools makes training more effective and keeps you and your dog safe.

Here is a list of the items you will need.

1. **Leash and Collar**—A sturdy leash and collar are basic items but important pieces of equipment. The leash helps you control

your dog during training, keeping it close and preventing it from wandering off. Make sure the collar fits well—not too tight, but not so loose that your dog can slip out of it. If your dog is used to wearing a harness instead of a collar, this will also work.

2. **Clicker**—A clicker is a small device that makes a clicking sound when pressed. It marks the exact moment your dog performs the desired behavior. Clicker training is a popular positive reinforcement method because it's precise and helps your dog quickly understand what you want them to do. During the clicker training process, your dog learns that a treat or praise is coming when they hear the clicker, making them eager to repeat the desired behavior.

Special Note: Not everyone wants to use a clicker for training, and that's perfectly fine. If you are one of those people, no worries! You can simply use the word "Yes" instead of the clicker sound. Your dog will quickly learn that hearing "Yes" means they've done something good, and a reward will follow - food, treat, or praise. Thus, your dog will want to repeat the behavior you want.

If you would like to include the use of a clicker but are unsure how I have included a section on Clicker Training in Chapter 3.

3. **Treats**—Treats are a must-have for positive reinforcement training. They reward your dog when it follows your cues or shows good behavior. However, I am aware that food rewards motivate not all dogs. If this describes your dog, you can substitute food treats with verbal praise, a good chin scratch, or a favorite toy. The key is to find what makes your dog happy and use that as a reward to encourage good behavior.

4. **High-Value Rewards**—High-value rewards are special treats or items that your dog finds particularly motivating and exciting. These rewards are more appealing than everyday kibble or common treats, making them highly effective for reinforcing desired behaviors during training sessions. More information on the use of High-value Rewards is covered in Chapter 3: Fundamental Skills.

5. **Treat Pouch**—It is especially handy to have a place to keep your treats, clicker, and other small items.

6. **Fake Snakes (Decoys)**—Using fake snakes during training helps simulate real-life encounters in a safe and controlled environment. These can be rubber or plastic snakes that look realistic enough to get your dog used to seeing snakes without any danger. Later in this book, you will find detailed instructions on how to set up training sessions and effectively use fake snakes to practice with your dog. For realistic-looking fake snakes, refer to the References section of this book for recommended sources.

7. **Shed Snake Skin)**—To add a scent element to your training, reach out to your local reptile store to see if they can provide you with the contents of the snake enclosure when they clean it, which should include shed snake skin. Be sure to store this material in an airtight container and use rubber gloves when handling it.

8. **Long Line**—A long line is a leash that can be 15 - 30 feet in length. It's useful for practicing the come when called (recall) cue and giving your dog more freedom to move while keeping it under control. A long line is particularly helpful in the advanced stages of training when you're teaching your dog to respond to

commands from a distance. These can be purchased affordably on Amazon.

9. **Water and Bowl**—Training sessions, especially outdoors and on hot days, can be tough on both you and your dog. Remember to have plenty of water on hand and take regular breaks to stay comfortable and focused during your training sessions.

10. **First Aid Kit** — Accidents can happen, even during training. A basic first aid kit for dogs should include:

* Bandages

* Antiseptic Wipes

* Tweezers

* Veterinarians or Pet Urgent Care Phone Number

Knowing you have a first aid kit available gives you peace of mind and ensures you're prepared for any unexpected situation.

Little Known Facts: Did you know that snakes don't have external ears like humans do? Instead, they have internal ear structures that allow them to sense vibrations through the ground.

CHAPTER 3: FUNDAMENTAL SKILLS
Building Basic Obedience

"POSITIVE REINFORCEMENT BUILDS A BRIDGE OF TRUST BETWEEN YOU AND YOUR DOG, ENCOURAGING LEARNING THROUGH LOVE AND REWARDS, NOT FEAR." KAREN PRYOR

Before teaching advanced training techniques, it's best to teach your dog basic obedience commands—just like teaching a child to swim in the shallow end of the pool before diving into the deep end.

Teaching your dog basic fundamental skills will set the stage for more complex commands and behaviors later. In this chapter, I cover the basic commands such as "sit," "stay," "come," and "leave it."

Mastering these basics not only makes everyday life with your dog easier but also ensures their safety and well-being. With patience, consistency, and positive reinforcement, you'll build a strong, trusting relationship with your dog that will make all future training smoother and more enjoyable. Let's get started on this important journey to a well-behaved and happy dog.

Note: *If your dog already consistently and reliably responds to the cues listed below, you can move on to Chapter 4.*

- **Come When Called or Recall Cue**

One of the most important commands you can teach your dog is to come when called. This command is important for your dog's safety and your peace of mind. When your dog reliably comes when called, you can prevent them from running into dangerous situations and ensure they stay close to you.

Training your dog to come when called takes patience, consistency, and lots of positive reinforcement.

* **Start in a Quiet Place**: Begin with no distractions, then slowly introduce distractions as your dog gets better at coming when you call it. Always call your dog in a happy, enthusiastic tone, and always reward it with treats, praise, or a favorite toy when it comes to you.

* **Make Coming Fun**: The aim is to make coming to you the best and most exciting thing for your dog. With time and practice, your dog will confidently and happily respond to the recall cue, knowing that good things happen when they obey.

* **Leave-It Cue:**

The "leave-it" cue is another important command that can keep your dog safe and make your life easier. Teaching your dog to leave something alone on command is incredibly useful, especially when they encounter something potentially dangerous or something you simply don't want them to have.

* **Start Small**: Begin with a treat in your hand. Show it to your dog,

then close your hand around it and say, "Leave it."

* **Wait for the Right Response**: Your dog will probably try to get at the treat. Be patient and wait until they lose interest or back away.

* **Reward the Behavior**: The moment your dog backs away or stops trying to get the treat, praise them and give them a different treat from your other hand. Doing so will teach them that good things happen when they leave something alone when told.

Note: High-value rewards are special treats or items that your dog finds particularly motivating and exciting. They are more appealing than everyday kibble or common treats, making them highly effective for reinforcing desired behaviors during training sessions.

Why Use High-Value Rewards

1. Increased Motivation: High-value rewards grab your dog's attention and encourage them to focus and work harder during training.

2. Positive Reinforcement: Using these rewards strengthens an association between good behavior and positive outcomes, making it more likely that your dog will repeat the behavior.

Tips for Using High-Value Rewards

* **Practice and Progress**: Repeat this until your dog consistently leaves the treat alone when you say, "Leave it." Then, gradually introduce more challenging scenarios, like placing the treat on the floor or using different objects.

- **Sit Cue:**

The command "Sit" allows you to control your dog's movements immediately. If you spot a snake or suspect one is nearby, telling your dog to sit can prevent them from moving closer and potentially getting bitten.

* **Get Their Attention:** Hold a treat close to your dog's nose to get their attention.

* **Raise the Treat**: Slowly lift the treat above your dog's head. As your dog follows the treat with its eyes, its bottom will naturally lower to the ground.

* **Say "Sit":** As soon as your dog's bottom touches the ground, say "sit" clearly and calmly.

* **Reward Immediately**: Give your dog the treat right away and praise them enthusiastically. Positive reinforcement helps them understand that sitting when asked leads to good things.

• **Focus Cue, aka Watch Me or Look Cues**:

The focus cue helps your dog pay attention to you instead of a potential danger, like a snake. The stay command is important because it helps prevent your dog from approaching or interacting with a snake.

* **Start with Basic Training**: Teach the focus cue in a quiet place with no distractions. Use treats or a favorite toy to get your dog to look at you when you say, "Watch me," "Focus," or "Look."

* **Practice in Different Settings**: Gradually practice the focus cue in different places with more distractions to make sure your dog can stay focused on you when you give the cue.

* **Reinforce Regularly**: Keep practicing the focus cue regularly to make sure your dog responds reliably, even in stressful situations.

• **Stay Cue:**

The stay command is a valuable tool for keeping your dog safe and well-behaved in various situations. Teaching your dog to stay in one place until you give a release command helps prevent them from running into danger, jumping on guests, or getting underfoot while you're busy.

* **Start with "Sit."** First, have your dog sit. The sit command provides a solid starting point for teaching the stay command.

* **Introduce Stay:** Once your dog is sitting, hold your hand out in front of you with your palm facing the dog and say "stay" in a firm but calm voice.

* **Take a Step Back:** Slowly take one step back, then quickly return to your dog before it has a chance to move out of the stay position.

* **Reward:** Immediately offer a reward by giving them a treat or anything your dog enjoys receiving.

* **Increase Duration and Distance**: Gradually increase the amount of time you ask your dog to stay and the distance you move away. Start with just a few seconds and a single step, then build up to longer durations and greater distances as your dog gets better at the command.

* **Use a Release Word**: Choose a release word like "Release," Free," or "Break" to let your dog know that they can move again. Always release your dog from the stay position before they move on their

own.

- **Clicker Training**: Incorporating a clicker when training your dog to avoid snakes can be highly effective for reinforcing positive behavior.

Start by familiarizing your dog with the clicker.

1. Gather a clicker and some high-value treats that your dog loves. Make sure you have a quiet environment with minimal distractions to begin the training.

2. Introduce the clicker by holding it in one hand and a treat in the other. Click the clicker and immediately give your dog a treat. Repeat this several times to help your dog associate the clicking sound with getting a treat.

3. Continue the process of clicking and treating in short sessions of 5 - 10 minutes. Do this a few times a day over several days. Your goal is to establish a clear connection in your dog's mind that click = treat.

4. Once you feel your dog has made the association, test it by clicking the clicker without showing the treat immediately. If your dog looks expectantly for a treat upon hearing the click, the association is successfully made. Reward your dog right after to reinforce this behavior.

5. Begin using the clicker during basic command training (e.g., sit, stay, come). Give the command, wait for your dog to perform the desired behavior, click, and then treat. This repetition will help your dog understand that the click marks the exact moment they did something right.

6. During snake avoidance training when your dog notices the fake snake but does not approach it, immediately click the clicker and reward your dog with a high-value reward.

7. Over time, your dog will learn to associate the sight of a snake with the need to avoid it, prompted by the clicker's sound and the subsequent reward.

For more information on Clicker Training, I suggest reading author Karen Pryor's book, "Don't Shoot the Dog!"

> **Little Known Fact:** *Did you know that some snake species, such as the Hognose Snake, will play dead when threatened? They will flip onto their backs, stick out their tongues, and even emit a foul smell to convince predators that they are not worth eating.*

◆ ◆ ◆

CHAPTER 4: RELATIONSHIP BUILDING

Understanding Your Dog's Needs

"POSITIVE REINFORCEMENT ISN'T ABOUT BRIBING YOUR DOG-IT'S ABOUT CREATING A RELATIONSHIP BASED ON MUTUAL RESPECT AND TRUST." - PAT MILLER

It's important to establish a solid foundation of trust and communication with your dog. In this chapter, I will guide you through the basics of building a strong relationship with your furry friend, which is the foundation for any successful training program.

Understanding Your Dog's Needs and Signals

The first step in building a relationship with your dog is understanding their needs and recognizing their communication signals. Dogs communicate through body language, such as tail wagging, ear positions, and eye contact. Learning to read these signs will help you understand when your dog is happy, anxious, or needs something from you.

Consistency is Key.

Consistency is the cornerstone of building trust.Whether it's feeding times, walks, or training sessions, keeping a regular schedule helps your dog know what to expect and that they can rely on you. This predictability builds a secure environment where your dog can thrive and be more receptive to training.

Positive Reinforcement

Positive reinforcement involves rewarding your dog for good behavior, which encourages them to repeat it. Treats, praise, or playtime are good rewards. This method not only strengthens your bond but also makes learning a joyful and fulfilling experience for your dog.

Effective Communication

Clear communication is important in training. When giving commands, use a firm yet gentle tone. Be concise and consistent with the words you choose for commands, such as "come," "stay," or "leave it." This clarity helps prevent confusion and ensures your dog understands what is expected of them. We'll cover these commands (cues) in more detail later in Chapter 5.

Patience and Understanding

Patience is essential when working with your dog. Each dog learns at their own pace, and it's important to give them time to understand and respond to training. Showing frustration or impatience can set back your progress, so always approach training sessions with a calm and positive demeanor.

Regular Practice

Regular practice is necessary for reinforcing learned behaviors. Short, frequent training sessions are more effective than occasional long sessions, which can tire your dog and reduce their ability to concentrate.

Building a Lasting Bond

The ultimate goal of foundation training is to develop a lasting bond based on mutual trust and respect. This strong connection will not only enhance your relationship but also significantly increase the effectiveness of more advanced training, such as snake avoidance techniques.

By prioritizing the foundation of trust and communication, you set the stage for a rewarding and effective training journey with your dog. This groundwork is not just about teaching commands —it's about creating a deep, understanding connection that will benefit both you and your dog in all aspects of life.

> *Little Known Fact: Did you know that snakes can control the amount of venom they inject during a bite? Some venomous snakes, like rattlesnakes, can choose to deliver a "dry bite," where no venom is injected, as a warning. This ability helps them conserve their venom for hunting prey and defending themselves against more serious threats.*

CHAPTER 5: SETTING THE STAGE

Simulating Real-Life Snake Encounters

" USING POSITIVE REINFORCEMENT TO TRAIN OUR DOG BUILDS A BOND OF TRUST AND MAKES LEARNING A JOYFUL EXPERIENCE FOR BOTH OF YOU." - ZAK GEORGE

Training your dog to avoid snakes involves creating set-ups that mimic real-life encounters in a safe and controlled environment.

Visit my Force Free Snake Avoidance Facebook page for actual training videos and discussion at: https://www.facebook.com/groups/forcefreetraining/

1. **Fake "Decoy" Snakes**: In a controlled environment like your backyard, place the fake snakes in different locations, making sure your dog does not see you handling or placing the decoy snakes in the yard.

Additional Tip: To make your training more effective, try attaching a 15-20-foot fishing line to the head of a decoy snake. Have a helper stand at a distance and gently pull on the line. Doing so will make the decoy snake appear alive and moving, adding a realistic touch to your training. Additionally, by downloading rattlesnake sounds on your smartphone and playing them during your session, you will be able to incorporate realistic sounds to your training.

2. **Giving the Cue:** Walk your dog on a leash, allowing it to notice one of the fake snakes. Immediately say the "leave it" command with a firm voice and move away from the area where you paced the fake snake. Reward your dog with treats and praise for moving away from the fake snake and following you.

Additional Tip: As soon as the dog sees the decoy snake, it's important to give the verbal cue - whether it's "Leave-it," "Snake," "Danger," or whichever cue you decide works best for you. Timing is key! If you give the cue too early, before the dog sees the decoy snake, or too late, after the dog has looked away, your dog might become confused about what to avoid. The cue must be given while the dog is looking directly at the decoy snake.

3. **Repetition is Key:** Continue step 2 with the remaining fake snakes you previously placed in the yard.

4. **Proofing the Behavior:** Attach a long lead, 10-20 feet, to your dog's collar and allow them some freedom to move independently from you. Have a helper gently tug on a fishing line attached to a decoy snake that is far enough away that the long lead will stop the dog from actually reaching the decoy. If the dog moves forward toward the decoy, immediately give the cue, "Leave-it," "Snake," "Danger," or whichever cue you decide works best for you. If the dog ignores the cue and continues to move toward the decoy, make sure the long lead is short enough that the dog can not reach the decoy.

5. **Changing the Environment:** Gradually add different environments to your training, like parks, hiking trails, or any place you would normally walk with your dog.

6. **Body Language:** Dogs are very in tune with their owner's body language and will mimic what they think the owner is feeling. While practicing with your dog, it's important to show a sense of danger with your body language and voice. You can do this by jumping back when your dog sees the fake snake and using an alarmed tone in your voice.

Part of what makes this Snake Avoidance training program unique is the use of non-verbal communication, also known as body language, by the dog's owner. Communication expert Paul Watzlawick writes, "We can not **not** communicate! Everything we do, think, and believe is communication." Around 60% of our communication is subconscious and non-verbal, 5% is conscious and non-verbal, and about 35% is verbal.

Roger Abrantes, a philosopher and evolutionary biologist, notes that "Focusing too much on behavior can make us forget the emotional part of our relationship with our dogs." He explains, "We use technology but have lost the habit of using ourselves. By combining the principles of ethology with behaviorism, we can learn how our body language affects our dogs' ability to respond.

Scientific studies suggest that dogs can pick up on emotions such as fear and or sense of danger communicated by humans through body posture and facial expressions. According to Patricia McConnell, author and animal behaviorist, "Your dog is most likely a far better observer than you are. We humans pay so much attention to verbal language that often interferes with our ability to see what's happening around us."

Little Known Fact: Did you know that some snakes can glide through the air? Certain species, like the paradise tree snake found in Southeast Asia, are capable of flattening their bodies and launching themselves from trees to glide distances of up to 100 meters. This remarkable ability helps them move between trees to escape predators or hunt for food.

SECTION 2   UNDERSTANDING AND PREVENTING SNAKEBITES

CHAPTER 6: STRATEGIES AND STATISTICS

Snakebite Statistics

While researching how many dogs are bitten by venomous snakes each year, I found conflicting information. One source reported that 15,000 dogs and cats suffer from snakebites annually. In contrast, other sources suggested the number could be even higher.

The difficulty in obtaining accurate statistics stems from several issues: many snakebites go unreported, and there is a lack of distinction between venomous and non-venomous bites.

Michael Schaer, DVN, a Professor of Veterinary Internal Medicine at the University of Flordia, explained this issue well. He said, "I don't believe we have a valid source of information on the actual numbers of dogs bitter or killed by snakes annually in the United States because there is no central data resource for this."

Snake-Proofing

Let's face it: there is no guaranteed way to snake-proof your yard, home, or the nature trails you and your dog enjoy. Guarding against the intrusion of snakes, not just rattlesnakes, is challenging. Still, there are some actions and precautions you can take.

While on nature trails, it's advisable to keep dogs on their leash. Veterinarians report that most dogs bitten by snakes were off-leash at the time of the bite. Choose wide trails and walk your dog in the middle of the path, away from the brush where snakes can hide.

By selecting wide trails, you're more likely to spot a sunning snake and avoid it than on narrow, brush-lined paths. Avoid tossing sticks or other objects for your dog to fetch. While playing fetch might seem fun, it's not worth the risk of your dog accidentally stepping on a hidden snake and getting bitten.

It's important to note that snakebite kits, despite their marketing claims, may not be as effective as they seem. In fact, they could do more harm than good. An article by Laura Johannes in The Wall Street Journal titled "Deadly Dilemma: Do Snakebite Kits Help?" highlights this concern, stating, "Scientists say the kits, which typically include suction devices and sometimes scalpels to drain the wound, may do more harm than good."

> *Little Known Facts: Did you know that some snake species, like the rattlesnake, give birth to live young instead of laying eggs?*

SECTION 3 INTERVIEWS
WITH THE EXPERTS

CHAPTER 7: DR. KAREN SEIBOLD, DVM, INTERVIEW

Snakebites are a serious concern for dog owners, especially those living in areas where venomous snakes are common. To provide expert insights on this topic, I interviewed Dr. Karen Seibold, DVM, a respected veterinarian with extensive experience in emergency animal care. In this interview, Dr. Seibold discusses the limitations of snakebite kits, effective measures for preventing snakebites, the role of the rattlesnake vaccine, and essential steps to take if your dog is bitten. Her advice is invaluable for ensuring the safety and well-being of your furry companions.

Interview with Dr. Karen Seibold, DVM

Q: Dr. Seibold, can you explain why snakebite kits are not recommended for treating snakebites in dogs?

Dr. Karen Seibold: Snakebite kits, which often include suction devices and sometimes scalpels, are generally not recommended because they can do more harm than good. The suction devices are supposed to remove venom from the wound. Still, studies have shown that they are ineffective and can actually cause additional tissue damage. Using a scalpel to cut the wound can also lead to severe complications, such as infections or increased venom absorption.

Q: What should a dog owner do if a snake bites their dog?

Dr. Seibold: If a snake bites your dog, the most important thing to do is to stay calm and get your pet to a veterinarian as quickly as possible. Do not try to cut the wound, suck out the venom, or apply ice. These actions can worsen the situation. Keep your dog as still and quiet as possible to slow the spread of venom, and seek immediate veterinary care.

Q: Are there any preventive measures dog owners can take to protect their pets from snakebites?

Dr. Seibold: Yes, several preventive measures can help reduce the risk of snakebites. First, always keep your dog on a leash when walking in areas where snakes are common. Having your dog on a leash allows you to have better control and prevent your dog from wandering into dangerous areas. Second, avoid walking your dog in tall grass, dense brush, or rocky areas where snakes may hide. Third, you can train your dog to avoid snakes using positive reinforcement techniques. Finally, consider speaking with your veterinarian about the rattlesnake vaccine, which can help reduce the severity of symptoms if your dog is bitten.

Q: Can you explain the role of the rattlesnake vaccine in snakebite prevention?

Dr. Seibold: The rattlesnake vaccine is designed to help a dog's immune system recognize and respond more quickly to rattlesnake venom. It does not provide complete protection, but it can reduce the severity of the reaction and give you more time to get your dog to a veterinarian. The vaccine is most effective when combined with other preventive measures, such as leash control and avoiding snake-prone areas.

Q: Is there anything else dog owners should know about snakebite treatment and prevention?

Dr. Seibold: The key is to be proactive and prepared. Educate yourself about the types of snakes in your area and their habitats so you can avoid them. Keep your yard clean and free of debris where snakes might hide. Always have a plan in place for quickly getting to a veterinarian in case of a snakebite. Remember, quick and calm action can make a significant difference in the outcome for your pet.

I want to thank Dr. Karen Seibold, DVM, for sharing her expertise with us. Her insights on diagnosing and treating venomous bites in pets are invaluable. I appreciate the time she took out of her busy schedule to help me, and my readers understand these important topics.

For my readers, remember to keep your pets safe and informed by visiting professionals like Dr. Seibold if your pet has a medical emergency or if you have any further questions or concerns about pet health.

> ***Little Known Fact:*** *Did you know that snakes use their tongues to "smell" the air, picking up scent particles that help them track prey?*

◆ ◆ ◆

CHAPTER 8: TOM DERR INTERVIEW

Snake encounters can be a serious concern for dog owners, particularly in areas where venomous snakes are common. To shed light on snake behavior and share valuable insights on snake safety, I sat down with Tom Derr, a seasoned expert with over 20 years of experience handling and rescuing snakes.

Tom, owner of Tom's Snakes and Rattlesnake Rescue in San Diego, California. In this interview, Tom discusses his journey into the world of snakes, offers practical advice for dog owners, and dispels common myths about these often misunderstood creatures. Join us for a fascinating conversation about snakes and how to keep your furry friends safe on nature trails.

DiLoreto: Thank you, Tom, for agreeing to meet with me this morning for this interview. I want to start by asking how you got started handling snakes.

Tom: Well, I guess it was 20 years ago when my daughter turned

15 and asked, "Dad, can I have a snake?" Lightning couldn't strike as fast as I said yes! As a kid, I always wanted a reptile, but my family only allowed dogs. So, my daughter got a snake, I got a snake, then she got another snake because her snake was lonely, and now I have 41 snakes.

DiLoreto: Are all your snakes non-venomous, or do you have venomous snakes as well?

Tom: I have venomous snakes. They are not harmful to humans, except for the ones I am rescuing. I have two Red Diamonds and a Southern Pacific right now that I was planning on releasing today, but that's not going to happen because of this interview and the fact that they didn't eat the food I gave them. I have to make sure they eat before I let them go. They will be released in Sycamore Canyon, away from human harm. The other snakes are classified as venomous but are rear-fanged, meaning they have to bite and chew for 10-15 minutes to envenomate. I don't know anyone who would let a snake chew on them for that long.

DiLoreto: (Laughing) Yes, I agree.

DiLoreto: Rear-fanged? That's a term I've never heard before; please explain.

Tom: It's like a garter snake. A garter snake is venomous; they have small rear fangs meant to immobilize their prey. Their venom is harmless to humans; you might get an allergic reaction if bitten, but nothing harmful.

DiLoreto: Kind of like a bee sting if you're allergic to bees?

Tom: Yes, if you were to have a reaction, that would be the worst-case scenario.

DiLoreto: That's fascinating. So, how did you get started in the rattlesnake rescue business?

Tom: Someone mentioned to Susan Nowicke, the President of the San Diego Herpetological Society, that they had a rattlesnake in their yard and didn't know what to do. Susan suggested they call me. I went over and took care of it; that was my first time rescuing a rattlesnake. I was a little nervous, but handling a snake is handling a snake; you have to use tools for venomous ones. Afterward, I thought, "Gee, I can get used to this!" From there, it just blossomed. Now, I'm teaching Animal Control cadets and San Diego Humane Society volunteers how to handle and remove venomous snakes humanely.

DiLoreto: Between your rescue business and teaching, you must stay very busy. Thank you for taking the time out of your schedule to speak with me today. I have gathered a few questions from students over the years and would like your opinion. I'll start with: Do rattlesnakes become angry and chase after people, dogs, or other animals to bite them?

Tom: There is no such thing as an angry rattlesnake or any other snake. They do not chase; they defend. Snakes prefer to be left alone, but if cornered, they will do whatever they can to protect themselves. Their first instinct is to rattle, hiss, and then bite —unless you surprise them. Snakes are virtually deaf; however, they do pick up vibrations in the ground and can feel footsteps as people approach. Dogs, on the other hand, walk softly, and their vibrations are not as easy to detect, especially if a snake is sunning itself. So, it is easy for a dog to startle a snake, which can cause the snake to strike/bite in defense. Snakes do not want to use their venom for defense if they don't have to. It takes a venomous snake a long time to regenerate venom after a bite, and venom is what they use to kill their prey and feed.

DiLoreto: I have heard that snakes are blind while shedding and thus more apt to bite. Is this true?

Tom: Yes. When they are "in the blue," their skin becomes opaque, their eyes are clouded over, and it is tough for them to see. They become scared and will lash out at anything they feel may threaten them.

DiLoreto: Does the term "in the blue" refer to shedding?

Tom: Yes. A snake that is about to shed is what we refer to as being "in the blue." Once the cloudiness clears up, within a week, the snake will start shedding.

DiLoreto: I have heard people say they found a nest of snakes. Do snakes live together in a nest?

Tom: The only snakes that really do that are garter snakes and rattlesnakes. Rattlesnakes will go to a den and hibernate or brumate during the winter months in areas that have a true winter. They do not hibernate here in Southern California; it's too warm. In regions like Colorado, rattlesnakes will hibernate.

I assume hibernation takes place before the first snow, but I honestly don't know.

DiLoreto: So, you are saying that rattlesnakes are present all year long in warmer climates like Southern California and that there isn't a rattlesnake season as I had thought?

Tom: No, there is no season for rattlesnakes in Southern California; they are out and about 24-7, 12 months a year, so you need to be careful. However, between November and March, we do see fewer rattlesnakes.

DiLoreto: If you are walking your dog and come upon a snake, how far can the snake strike or jump, for lack of a better word, towards you and your dog?

Tom: 2/3 to 3/4 of their body length if the snake is coiled, and a little less if it's not coiled. If you encounter a snake sunning itself on a path, pick up some soft dirt and toss it at the snake. Let it know you are there, and often it will scurry away. If not, you may need to find an alternate route.

Thank you, Tom Derr, for sharing your extensive knowledge and experiences with us today. Your tips on snake safety and handling are incredibly useful for anyone living in areas where snakes are common.

For my readers, always remember to keep an eye out for snakes and follow the safety advice shared by experts like Tom. If you encounter a snake, stay calm and contact a professional like Tom to ensure it's handled safely.

Little Known Fact: Did you know that snakes can dislocate their jaws to swallow prey much larger than their heads?

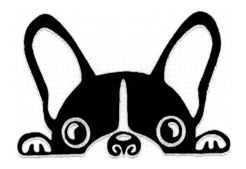

SECTION 4 ACTUAL TRAINING PHOTOS

Photo: Orange Rubber Decoy Snake by Training Staff

Photo: Snake Avoidance Training Team by Training Staff

Photo: Decoy Rattle Snake with Shedded Snake Skin in Background by Training Staff

Photo: Golden Retriever Snake Avoidance Class by Training Staff

Dog Avoiding Decoy Snakes After After Training Class

Decoy Snake

An excellent example of how dog owners should demonstrate that snakes mean danger - by running away.

Note: For more photos, videos, and discussion on keeping dogs safe in areas where snakes might be present, visit my Facebook group at https://www.facebook.com/groups/forcefreetraining/

Little Known Facts: *Did you know that the skin of a snake is covered in scales made of keratin, the same material found in human fingernails and hair?*

◆ ◆ ◆

SECTION 5 SNAKE BITES - IMAGES MAY BE DISTURBING

Dr. Karen Seibold, DVM. Dr. Seibold provided the following images. Established in 1996 in Escondido, CA, Dr. Seibold owns Animal Urgent CarShe lectures both locally and nationally on diagnosing and treating venomous bites in dogs and cats. Dr.

Seibold is also a Board Member for Venom Week, a human toxicology group, and has been a Diplomate of the American College of Veterinary and Critical Care since 1998.

Note: Dogs get bit in the face when they try to smell the snake.

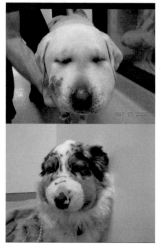

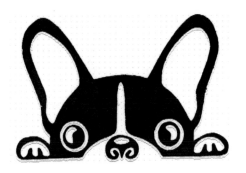

SECTION 6 VACCINATIONS AND MEDICAL TREATMENT

CHAPTER 9: EMERGENCY MEDICAL TREATMENT

When a venomous snake bites a dog, it's a serious medical emergency that requires immediate attention. Knowing the steps to take can significantly impact the outcome and potentially save your dog's life.

This chapter will guide you through the necessary actions, the types of treatments available, and what to expect during the recovery process.

I will refer to expert advice from reputable sources such as the American Veterinary Medical Association (AVMA), VCA Animal Hospitals, PetMD, and the Merck Veterinary Manual.

Immediate Actions

1. **Stay Calm:** According to the American Veterinary Medical Association (AVMA), when a dog is bitten by a venomous snake,

the first and most important step is to stay calm. Your dog will pick up on your anxiety, which can worsen their condition.

2. **Keep Your Dog Still:** The AVMA also advises keeping your dog still, as movement can accelerate the spread of venom through the bloodstream,

3. **Identify the Snake:** If it is safe to do so, try to remember the snake's color and size, or if possible, take a photo using your cellphone. This information can assist the vet in identifying the type of venom.

4. **Avoid Home Remedies:** The American Veterinary Medical Association - First Aid for Snake Bites cautions not to attempt to suck out the venom, cut the bite, or apply ice. These methods can do more harm than good.

Transporting Your Dog to the Vet

* **Limit Movement:** Carry your dog if possible or use a stretcher. (VCA Hospitals - Snake Bite in Dogs**).**

* **Call Ahead:** Inform the veterinary clinic that you are on your way and provide details about the incident. This information will allow the vet to prepare the necessary antivenom and equipment. VCA Hospitals - Snake Bite in dogs).

Note: It is a good idea to program your cellphone with your veterinary clinic or the nearest animal urgent care number. Also, note that not all Veterinarians carry a supply of antivenom on hand, so it is best to clarify this before making an unnecessary trip.

Veterinary Treatment

1. **Assessment and Stabilization:** The veterinarian will conduct a physical examination, monitor vial signs, such as blood pressure and help flush the venom from the system.

* According to PetMD, the vet will assess the severity of the bite and the dog's overall condition to determine the appropriate course of action (PetMD - Snake Bites on Dogs).

 * **Vial Signs Monitoring:** Blood pressure, heart rate, and respiratory rate will be closely monitored.

Intravenous (IV) Fluids: Administered to maintain blood pressure and help flush the venom from the system.

2. **Antivenom Administration:**

* **Identification of Venom:** Based on the snake's description, the appropriate antivenom will be selected.

* **Dosage:** The amount of antivenom needed depends on the size of the dog and the severity of the bite. The antivenom neutralizes the venom's effects and is most effective when given within the first few hours after the bite.

3. **Pain Management:**

* Analgesics: Pain relief is given for the comfort and recovery of your dog. The vet will administer pain medications to manage discomfort.

4. Treatment of Complications:

* **Antibiotics:** Snake bites can introduce bacteria, leading to infection; antibiotics may be prescribed to prevent or treat infections.

* **Anti-Inflammatories:** To reduce swelling and tissue damage at the bite site.

 Blood Transfusions: In severe cases where the venom has caused significant blood clotting issues or anemia, a blood transfusion might be necessary.

Monitoring and Recovery

1. **Follow-Up Appointments:** Regular check-ups will be necessary to monitor your dog's recovery and address any ongoing issues.

2. **Wound Care:** Continue to clean the bite area as instructed by the ver and watch for signs of infection such as redness, swelling, or discharge.
3. **Activity Restriction:** Limit your dog's activity to prevent stress on the recovering body. Follow the vet's advice on when it is safe to resume normal activities.

4. **Nutrition:** Provide a balanced diet to support the healing

process. Your vet may recommend specific foods or supplements to aid recovery.

CHAPTER 10: SNAKEBITE VACCINE PROS AND CONS

Snakebites can be a serious threat to dogs, particularly in regions where venomous snakes are prevalent. One preventative measure that has gained attention is the snakebite vaccine for dogs.

This chapter will explore the benefits and drawbacks of this vaccine, helping pet owners make informed decisions about their dog's health and safety.

Understanding the Snakebite Vaccine

The snakebite vaccine, aims to create an immune response in dogs that can neutralize snake venom. The vaccine is designed to buy time for the dog to receive medical treatment, potentially reducing the severity of the venom's effects.

Pros of the Snakebite vaccine:

1. Extended Time for Treatment:

* The primary benefit of the snakebite vaccine is that it can extend the time available to get the dog to a veterinary clinic after

a bite. This extended time can be critical in rural or remote areas where immediate veterinary care may not be readily available.

2. Reduced Severity of Symptoms:

* Vaccinated dogs may experience less severe symptoms from a snake bite. The vaccine can help reduce the amount of tissue damage and pain, improving the dog's chances of full recovery.

3. Cost-Effective Preventative Measure:

* Compared to the cost of emergency antivenom treatment, the snakebite vaccine is relatively inexpensive, thus making it a cost-effective way for pet owners to mitigate the risk of snakebites.

4. Increased Peace of Mind:

* Knowing that their dog has some level of protection against snakebites can provide pet owners with peace of mind, especially in areas with high snake activity.

Cons of the Snakebite Vaccine:

1. Limited Scope of Protection:

* The vaccine is specifically designed for the Western Diamondback Rattlesnake. While there may be some cross-protection, it does not guarantee immunity against bites from other venomous snakes, such as coral snakes, cottonmouths, or other rattlesnake species.

2. Possible Side Effects:

* Like any vaccine, the snakebite vaccine can have side effects. These may include swelling at the injection site, lethargy, and allergic reactions. Severe reactions are rare by possible.

3. False Sense of Security:

* There is a risk that pet owners might become complacent, relying solely on the vaccine for protection. It is important to remember that the vaccine is not a substitute for prompt medical treatment in the event of a snakebite.

4. Need for Regular Boosters:

* The vaccine requires regular booster shots to maintain its effectiveness, creating an ongoing cost and commitment for pet owners.

5. **Variable Efficacy:**

* The effectiveness of the vaccine can vary from dog to dog. Some dogs may develop a strong immune response, while others may have limited protection.

Veterinary Perspectives

Veterinary experts have differing opinions on the snakebite vaccine. Some vets recommend it for dogs that live in or frequently visit high-risk areas, citing its potential to reduce the severity of snakebites. Others are more cautious, emphasizing that the vaccine is not a foolproof solution and should be used in conjunction with other preventative measures, such as avoiding snake-prone areas and undergoing snake avoidance training.

References:

* American Veterinary Medical Association (AVMA). "Snakebite Prevention and Treatment for Pets." Retrieved from AVMA.

* VCA Animal Hospitals. "Snakebite in Dogs." Retrieved from VCA Hospitals.

* PetMD. "Snake Bite Vaccine for Dogs." Retrieved from PetMD.

* Merck Veterinary Manual. "Snakebite in Animals." Retrieved

from Merck Veterinary Manual.

SECTION 7 IDENTIFYING SNAKE TYPES

CHAPTER 11: VENOMOUS SNAKES:

Characteristics and Regions

Venomous Snakes Found in the United States, Canada, and North America.

Image: Eastern Diamonback Rattlesnake by GlobalIP/IStock Photo

Eastern Diamondback Rattlesnake (Crotalus adamanteus)

* **Characteristics:** Large, heavy -Bodied with diamond-shaped patterns along the back, and a distinctive rattle at the tail end.

* **Region:** Southeastern United States, including Flordia, Georgia, and the Carolinas.

Image: Copperhead Snake by Jenniveve84/iStock Photo

Copperhead (Agkistrodon contortix)

* Characteristics: Medium-sized, with a copper-red head and hourglass-shaped bands on a tan or light brown body.

* Region: Eastern and Central United States, from the southern New England area to Texas.

Image: Western Diamondback Rattlesnake by Johnaudrey/iStockphoto

Western Diamondback Rattlesnake

Characteristics: Heavy-bodied with diamond patterns, a rattle at the tail, and a stripe running diagonally from the eye to the mouth.

Region: Southern United States, including Arizona, New Mexico, and Texas, extending into northern Mexico.

Image: Coral Snake by Chase 'aimulis/iStock photo

Coral Snake (Micrurus spp.)

Characteristics: Brightly colored with red, yellow, and black bands. Notable for the rhyme "Red touch yellow, kill a fellow; red touch black, friend of Jack."

Region: Southeastern United States, including Florida and the Gulf Coast states, as well as parts of Central and South America.

Image: Mojave Rattlesnake by Steve Byland/iStock photo

Mojave Rattlesnake (Crotalus scutulatus)

Characteristics: Similar to other rattlesnakes, but known for it's potent venom, often featuring greenish hues and diamond patterns.

Region: Southwestern United States, particularly in the Mojave Desert regions of California, Nevada, Arizona, and Utah.

REFERENCES

Image Credits:

All snake images are used with permission from iStock Photo. Specific credits are provided with each image.

Training References:

Bradshaw, J. (2011). *Dog Sense: How the New Science of Dog Behavior Can Make You a Better Friend to Your Pet*. Basic Books Publishing.

Castellano, J. (2016). Rattlesnake Avoidance Training Aims to Save Dogs' Lives. Retrieved from http://www.sltrib.com/home/4176085-155/rattlesnake-avoidance-training-aims-to-sa.

Cattet, J. (2014). Is Your Body Language Helping or Confusing Your Animal? Retrieved from http://blog.smartanimaltraining.com/2014/06/02/is-your-body-language-helping-or-confusing-your-animal/.

Dunn, T.J. Snake Bites and Dogs. Retrieved from http://www.petmd.com/dog/care/evr_dg_snake_bites_and_dogs.

Johannas, L. (2009). Deadly Dilemma: Do Snake-Bite Kits Help? *The Wall Street Journal*.

Mienk, A. (2011). *The Invisible Link to Your Dog*. Cadmon Publishing.

Rooney, S. Training Methods and Owner-Dog Interactions: Links with Dog Behavior and Learning Ability. *Applied Animal Behavior Science*, vol 132.

Stilwell, V. *Train Your Dog Positively*. Crown Publishing.

The University of Lincoln. (2016). A Man's Best Friend: Study Shows Dogs Can Recognize Human Emotions. *ScienceDaily*. Retrieved April 21, 2017, from www.sciencedaily.com/releases/2016/01/160112214507.htm.

Dr. Major L. Broddiker. Rattlesnake Control Methods. Retrieved from https://www.colorado.gov/pacific/sites/default/files/Rattlesnake%20Control%20Methods.pdf.

Medical Treatment References:

American Veterinary Medical Association (AVMA). "First Aid for Snake Bites." Retrieved from AVMA.

VCA Animal Hospitals. "Snake Bite in Dogs." Retrieved from VCA Hospitals.

PetMD "Snake Bites on Dogs." Retrieved from PetMD.

Merck Veterinary Manual "Snakebite in Animals." Retrieved from Merck Veterinary Manual.

Suggested Materials:

I purchase my decoy snakes from this website: https://shop.thebigzoo.com/collections/all/rubber-snakes.

ABOUT THE AUTHOR

Penny Diloreto

In addition to her work on snake avoidance, Penny has authored several highly acclaimed training books available on Amazon.

"Potty Perfection: A Proven System for Puppy House Training" (https://a.co/d/cWHp5nu) is a practical, step-by-step guide that ensures a smooth transition for both the pet and the owner during the housetraining process.

"The ABCs of Dog Training: Mastering Antecedent, Behavior, and Consequence," https://a.co/d/4ShuKr3, breaks down the fundamentals of dog training into simple, easy-to-follow steps. This book is perfect for both new dog owners and those looking to refine their training techniques, focusing on understanding and effectively communicating with dogs.

Penny DiLoreto's unwavering commitment to sharing her knowledge and passion for dog training is evident in her books, workshops, and online content.

ADDITIONAL BOOKS BY THE AUTHOR

The ABCs of Dog Training: Mastering Antecedent, Behavior and Consequence.

READER REVIEW:

Easy and Helpful Read! - As a dog owner striving to understand and effectively train my pet, I was thrilled to come across "The ABC's of Dog Training" by Penny DiLoreto. This book is not just a training manual; it's a deep dive into the science of dog behavior. The clarity with which the concepts of Antecedent, Behavior, and Consequence (ABC) are explained is truly remarkable. Diloreto demystifies the psychological triggers behind a dog's actins, making it easy to even beginners to grasp and apply these concepts. - N2H2O

Potty Perfection: A Proven System For Puppy House Training.

READER REVIEW:

This book is like having a savvy dog trainer right in your pocket. It's chock-full of tips and tricks to make potty training your furry friend a breeze. Whether you're a newbie or a seasoned pet parent, this book's got your back with step-by-step instructions and real-life scenarios. Plus, it goes beyond just potty training, diving into the science behind how puppies learn and behave. - Jan A. Nesbit

Made in the USA
Columbia, SC
29 July 2024

39454558R00044